Lynda Tavakoli

THE BOILING POINT FOR JAM

ARLEN
HOUSE

The Boiling Point for Jam

is published in 2020 by
ARLEN HOUSE
42 Grange Abbey Road
Baldoyle, Dublin 13, Ireland
Phone: 00 353 86 8360236
arlenhouse@gmail.com
arlenhouse.blogspot.com

978–1–85132–249–7, *paperback*

Distributed internationally by
SYRACUSE UNIVERSITY PRESS
621 Skytop Road, Suite 110
Syracuse, NY 13244–5290
Phone: 315–443–5534
Fax: 315–443–5545
supress@syr.edu
syracuseuniversitypress.syr.edu

poems © Lynda Tavakoli, 2020

Typesetting by Arlen House

Cover image by Emma Barone

CONTENTS

THE BOILING POINT FOR JAM

KITCHEN COMFORTS

Resistance hugs the small kitchen,
hiding secrets amongst
gloomy cupboard space,
post-war austerity brooding
on strained shelves.

Empty jars wheedle their
glass weight into the wood,
its protest stifled only
by the hum of a fridge –
a magic fridge procreating
eggs by the dozen,
their longevity evidenced only
by an absence of feathers.

Plastic bags like artificial flower heads
scrunch in hidden corners
anticipating usefulness –
receptacles for ashes and potato skins,
swarf from box hedges,
odd bits of wool waiting for the charity shop.

An Easter cactus prospers on a sill
heedless of the pills that leave
their-tell-tale tips above the parched soil
where she drove them in.

This is the place she planned her day,
where through a kitchen window
the dulled reminders of her life
still resonated in the ordinary –
a rose she'd slipped
blushing the oil tank in summer,
the remnants of a forgotten meal,
animal fodder on the lawn.

Nothing went to waste,
not even the birdsong
wakening her at dawn
that somehow hummed upon her lips
for the remainder of the day.

DEAD DOG

In a unit for the mentally infirm
I offer you my love in the form of a dog
so lifelike you expect its tail to wag
or its soft muzzle to crinkle into smiles.
It's a collie – a she, a Daisy-dog to give comfort
when your night-walls are soughed by the demented
and God has forgotten the numbered password
at your door.

I have seen the woman with her baby many times,
its doll head bobbing on her ribs,
the lullaby that sings upon her tongue
a comfort only to the bogus child
immured within those skinned and skinny limbs.
She walks the ward oblivious to all but
what contentment comes before
the longer shreds of darkness that will
swallow up her memory whole.

So I tender you my good intent –
this spurious gift I think will link an alien present
with the familiar past but even then,
with all that has been lost to you,
you recognise its falsity.
'That's a dead dog,' you say,
the words raged from that part of you
still holding on and holding on.

Is This What I Do?

On a corridor of fresh-painted magnolia
sunbeams stroke from Velux windows
onto freckled carpets, while a television
talks too loudly to itself in someone's room.

I find you sleeping, head sagged
as on a mis-hung coathanger, hair,
just brushed, still full of wartime curls,
a legacy that did not pass itself to me.

I say your name, see the reluctant
wakening of your eyes, the disappointment
you had not slept your way to heaven.
You have told me this before.

Today we talk of blue dresses and funerals
and how you love my coat, and how
you love my coat, the colour redolent
of something already scudding out of view.

You ask me now if this is what you do,
just sit and wait, and wait and sit,
the resignation in your voice
the hardest thing for me to bear.

For in this room, that thief of time
has measured out its false remembrance in
the ticking of a clock, as the past becomes the present
and the present loiters somewhere in the past.

DONE

Death bleaches into bone,
the smell of oldness
secreting in the folds
of laundered sheets.

Old   Old   Old

Your face reflected
in the greying wood of trees
and origami limbs
a plicature of
skeleton and skin.

You ask,
'Is someone dying here?'
and to the silence add,
'You're good. I'll keep you,'

the words
your parting gift –

the love you left.

DUCK EGG BLUES

My father roasted them,
their soft blue
smothered in the ashes
of a spent day,
later buttered and salted
in mugs glaze-crackled
and chipped with the history
of generations.

The peat-smoke taste
waits on my tongue,
remembering,
a flush-faced girl
hunkered by the hearth
and a childhood's riches
stored within the promise
of a single shell.

WHAT WE WASTE

In wheel-chaired anticipation they gather
and I will sing 'Carrickfergus' for them,
this posse of souls,
eyes eternity-filled already,
but no matter. It does not matter.

I find a note, difficult with
the range of the song, and start to sing,
transported to a time of used to be,
when music rinsed my childhood
with begrudging sweetness.

Afterwards somebody shouts,
'Will you not sing "Carrickfergus" for us?'
as though the song had been already
chewed up, regurgitated
and made ready for repeat.

So I start again, not minding,
at peace with an audience
who cannot criticise
or hold the notes in place
for longer than a blink.

And in a room not far away
my mother and sister
with the open door of my throat
swallowing their silence with song,
and my mother's whisper, like filigree,

'That's her. She used to have such a beautiful voice.'

MOVING DAY

I moved my mother
into our dining room,
her presence boxed and waiting
for the final shift
to a shed outside.

The pain of her absence
stuttered my will
to let her go,
black bags remaining empty
of the detritus
I could not throw away –

shopping lists on paper scraps,
repeated phone numbers
written in her tiny
disappearing hand
all about the house,

'just in case.'

GONE

Even now your warmth tortures me
though you decided for yourself
to leave without us being there.

And me, wishing you back,
able only to stare
at the hollow of your throat
to a pulse extinguished
suddenly to stillness.

For in the end we are simply left
with sadnesses,
their shadows shocking
as they cross the sun,
while in between remains
the light that says life carries on,

only because it does.

WORDS

At fifteen he left school – my father –
then a boy, countrified and green,
setting out for lands beyond
the island of his birth.
What he knew was the call
of curlews across a lough,
the smell of rain teasing its way over a bog,
or the hard knocks it took
for being tenth of a litter of ten.

Later, when time had softened his edges
and that bright mind of his
no longer grieved the absence of opportunity,
he sought solace in words,
their tiny print etched like the footprints of ants
on the *Chambers's Twentieth Century Dictionary*
waiting on our scullery shelf,
its brown paper cover wrapped like a familiar cardigan
around pages thin as rice paper.

At tea times my father consumed words
the same way he ate the food on his plate –
words like gelid and linch,
sympodium and ruderal, memoriter and treen,
each one explored with tenderness of thought
and the feathered touch of a big man's fingertips.

It wasn't only the meanings he sought
but the way they were pronounced,
how they resonated on the tongue,
their spelling, their etymology,
their simple and joyous surprises!
These were his absent education
and means of passing on to us
what he felt he must have lost.

My father, normally a man of few words,
offering them up to us like something unexplored
and waiting only for the joy of their release.

MY BOY

Sometimes at night
when the house was in sleep
I slipped into your room
to catch the shadows
of your breathing
in the empty air.

And no one knew
except perhaps
those ample-breasted girls
with air-brushed smiles
who spied from calendars
of teenage boys' desires.

How cruel then
the turn of time
that stole your innocence
and left behind
within these lonely walls
a place where only silent
heartbeats live.

For now your breathing
whispers shadows
in another's ear
and I am forced to let you go,
your journey into adulthood complete –

my lovely boy.

LILY'S PLACE

Its two-up, two-down walls have hunched
their mortared backs,
a poach of creepers too long now in the making
for any redemption.
Outside, a fence she painted green, always 'forest'
one year, 'fern' the next,
leans a last resistance to neglect it did not ask for,
nor expect.
And here is me, standing at her closed front door,
remembering.

A Rayburn stove, born the same year as me,
I was always told,
will still stand sentry in the parlour, a freckling
of black spit on the carpet,
reminders of its choked out innards and too many
overlooked close-calls.
But there will be a bible there to save her, and the tracts,
and church envelopes,
and the charity appeals that kept on coming every time she
sent them more.

There's the cuckoo clock above the chair she sat in,
its voice lost to overuse
sometime in 1966, its game little body
continuing to poke a presence
for years afterwards. There will be that oldie smell
that sucked into my child's bones
and made a home there
even when I left.
And there will be the scullery of coldness and oldness
and nothing much besides.

If I take the stairs my feet might pause
upon the second tread,
a thinning carpet bulging banknotes
(for emergencies or birthdays),
and any self-respecting burglar's dream. Follow, then,
the spoor of
daisied paper weeping from the walls and find
her tiny bedroom, long ago
resigned to her frugality – a bed, a chest of drawers,
a quiet harbour for the soul.

And here is me, standing at her closed front door,
remembering
the moment when she asked me where she was
and who was I.
Remembering the day I closed this old front door
and turned the lock.
But most of all remembering, in that other place,
the time I asked her
what she thought about and she said, home.

ROUND THE ROUND O

We walk the curves of the Round O
on Sunday afternoons,
the slow shift of sandals
seeping my mother's
tired years into the gravel.

There is only the lake here now
and an empty coffee house
long boarded up and dead,
a swimming pool
weed-choked and indistinct,
concrete belly slimed
by its curse of neglect.

We have become the water's outer skin,
my mother and I,
skimming its surface like stones
until the final suck pulls us under,
unlayering the bruises of our love.

Regrets secrete themselves,
unaware of what will come
but now it is enough to simply know
the comfort of her shuffling feet
and hear her say,
'Remember to feed the dog
when we get home'

and me thinking of her cat
waiting there on the sill
behind a netted windowpane.

THE BIG FREEZE

They were found together,
limbs stretched like starched shirts
abandoned on a washing line,
fingers, stalacto-stalagmites of frozen touch.
Winter had finally seized them,
their black crow cloaks no match for the worst
whiteout in a hundred years.

In stories they were witches,
two sisters hiding their eccentricities
in the anonymity of a bog,
magic spells and caldrons
fodder for tale-tellers around
the open fires of my childhood.

But hiding in the pinked dapple
of a rogue beech I had watched them once,
their meagre chatter bouncing off each other
like the sonar of a bat, their faces soft with kindnesses
as one by one they picked words from the earth
and rested them upon the other's mouth
like a coming melt of snow.

KISSED

I am fifteen,
smoking in a hay barn
with a boy I hardly know,
the day stretched behind us,
the fall of evening
passing shadows through gaps
in corrugated tin.

It is madness,
this risk too far,
as I taste the smoke-spill
on his mouth and wonder
at the old man's dog
outside on the concrete,
untroubled by the gathering dusk.

A MATTER OF EXPEDIENCY

Replete from the blessing of Irish summers
a water butt hugged the corner of our gable wall,
spittle mouth gawped skyward,
its lurking tongue thirsty for rain
to swell an ever hungry belly.

Mother's soft-water voice spoke fondly of it,
as though the contents were some holy thing
only adults had the wherewithal to see.
She did not seem to notice a carnivorous intent,
its saturated bodies floundering
on the surface of that cunning cemetery.

But none at school owned hair like mine,
my country head a lustre jug of dead
and living matter, shiny as my mother's promise
when she ladled, every Sunday afternoon,
that smarting deluge over my reluctant head.

THE PLEASURE GARDENS

The cast-iron gate of the park
clenches its bite,
a corroded dental brace
of rusted teeth and gum,
while a padlock hangs
like an abandoned scrotum
from its chain.

Somewhere behind,
swings are strangled
in their ropes, nooses
tightening on gulps of wind,
and on the dry concrete
a scuff of children's feet
ruts an imprint like a scar.

On the bandstand
litter dances out a
tumbleweed routine
across the stage,
its missing audience betrayed
by spills of spat butts
underneath the boards.

Welcome to the Pleasure Gardens,
Northern Ireland 1963,
where the only game in town
on Sunday is to pick a lock
or wait until tomorrow
when it's free to sample
its more prurient delights.

CHANGING GEARS

Me between the cradle of his knees,
a chew of steering wheel on puppy fat,
eyes round as sixpences from the dare
of a wide-eyed lane, my hand
parcelled in the plump pads
of his own big hand churning up the gears.

A decade later, when he taught me
properly to drive, that passenger seat
roar of his to brake – Brake!
An impatience of aging, the superiority of youth,
the vow to my mother to never get inside
a car with that man ever again.

There were things I never fully understood.
His sudden coming home too early in the day,
work keys tossed, their uses temporarily obsolete,
the threat of being 'burnt out or leave'
still thundering behind the surrender in his eyes,
staff cars spared only because he'd done as he was told.

Then the serious stuff of family business
steered from the office of a bruised oak desk,
the writing of cheques for our education –
be frugal, be kind, be fair, and that thing he knew most
how to give away, chiselled from his own unspoken past,
the sense of what was right and what was wrong.

Later, a slow shrinkage of the father we knew,
hurrying slowly, his neck curved as though
he'd spent a lifetime ducking under doors.
And the final humiliation – you must not drive –
filching his freedom and swallowing up
the grim shadow of the road that lay ahead.

But there he is, with the wind salting his cheeks,
an elbow slack on an open window ledge,
spills of sunshine kaleidoscoping the windscreen.
Now he has all the time in a very long time,
freewheeling the highway and raking up the gears,
finding that endings can sometimes
be beginnings in disguise.

BOW SAW

It waited for them on a nail in the woodshed,
a yawn of bottom teeth sharpened and honed
through generations of family labour.
Often I had watched my father
and older brother at work – the saw's heel and toe
ripping their rhythm across each grain a steady kerf apart,
the teeth's angle easing a perfect bite into the wood.

Something in me longed for it –
touch that was not a touch between parent and child,
an unspoken connection singing through the blade
into the other's hand like the words of a hymn.
But when my father finally let me try
I was no good for it, the push and pull of muscle
a magic of timing as alien to me then as getting old.

So now it hangs upon another nail,
a starved mouth of spitted teeth
spilling like sawdust onto the garage floor,
waiting for the too late thrust of my regret.

A WEIGHT OF DUST

She perches on our parents' bed
dusting words from books
when she should be
dusting.
Green eyes flit saccades across pages,
hoarding books on shelves
in the attic of her brain,
while ornaments hold court
to words that leak their meanings
through the movement of her lips.

Years later I would wonder at
the weight of knowledge
magicked from my sister's weekly chore,
remembering only the emergence
of her Sunday smile
and those dusty rooms where
stories shed their skins in settled particles
on listening window sills.

MURDER IN THE FIRST

The first time I tried to kill my sister we were in a bath,
the vague drift of our mother's hum
scenting through an open window from the garden.
The water's tepidness sloshed a small tsunami
between our spooned bodies, the combined grime of us
tide-marking a plimsoll line around the white enamel.

A spiky spine of bones protruded like the carcass
of some ancient stegosaurus down her back,
each vertebra flinching as I beakered water
on her skinny shoulders from the tap.
Not hot enough, she said, her seniority then
a valid reason for a younger sister to comply.

In bed that night I prayed to Jesus,
or whoever else would listen, that she'd live,
and my punishment would take into account
the archipelago of beauty I had fondly
scorched like a tattoo upon her naked skin,
and that I'd kindly left for her to keep.

Initiation By Fire

I'd been smoking proper cigarettes
behind our garage for years
before persuading her to succumb;
until now my sister's
goody-two-shoes veneer
always a deterrent against
my naïve blatancy.

So we waited for an empty house,
where evidence of her sin might
permeate a smoke-choked hearth,
and like our Santa letters
from the past, fly the chimney,
spattering cancer dust upon
our unsuspecting red tiled roof.

The newspaper spooled itself
sausage-fat between my fingers,
the day's headline briefly
inked within the rollup layers
of a virgin cigarette.
My spit secured the sides
and sealed the deal.

I let the match lick
over the sheared tip,
an ochre flame chewing
into airless layers
of yesterday's news,
grasping for words
to ignite its unforgiving grip.

It's like jumping into
a cold swimming pool, I said,

you have to do it all at once,
and when the smoke sampled
that first sweet taste of lung
I watched my sister drown
in the smouldering ash of my deceit.

WAR AND WANT

The dust is first, always,
before the sun crisps the skin
or sand moulds molten heat
between our toes,
there is always and ever
the dust to welcome us.

No orifice hides from its gritting,
no spit or piss protected from
the chaff of misted rock
that scrapes its way inside,
the powdered bones of the dead
ghosting their revenge.

Yet in the sleeping hours
I still dream of you,
beautiful even in the way
that angels are
who smile their enigmatic smiles
among the bloodied spoils of war.

For I feel the rise and fall of us
lusting my nights like the killings
that also lust my days,
and will you forgive
my need for you
when you learn
of my hunger for both?

But you are not to know
these soldier thoughts
that scar my days and nights –
for the thing that was first is last, always,
disintegrating again to the fineness of dust
welcoming us all.

GAME ON

In Syria the shooters
choose themes for target practice,
a living video game
of entertainment for the week.

On Saturday it's chins,
anything below the nose, above the neck,
and rifle sights explore
a quivered lip
as points deduct for errors –
cheeks and ears are left
for Sunday's sport.

On Monday, it's the old,
their leech-peeled progress
over desert skin the easier to track,
points deducted for impairment
but added for an outright kill.

On Tuesday, pregnant women.
Two for the price of one (but scarce)
with double points for primary executions,
only if you're in the zone.

On Wednesday, barrel metal
rests on gaping sills,
trigger fingers slack
for mobiles phoning home
while someone calculates the points
but lets the stretcher bearers
live upon a whim.

Thursday's dawn will drone
unblinking and unlit,

sheltering the snipers'
bull's-eyed sleep from heavenly foe.
Anonymous the joystick thumb
that strokes its target
from behind a foreign screen,
one final arbitrary theme,
the sum of all its parts,
no worse, no better
than what's gone before.

Friday now and Holy Day.
Notch up the scores
before the credits start to roll
and silence sucks its permadeath of souls
into the black hole of a VDU.

ALTERED

Bullet holes scab forgotten walls
while the hush of the dead
still rinses through your bones
with the coldering of war.

Here you are, returned,
but altered in a way
no body has a right to be,
seeking comfort for your damaged soul
in the benevolence of strangers.

You ask what we can know of war,
we, who view its consequences
safe within our homes,
fingering the *on* and *off*
as easily as a child can raze
an image from a screen.

We cannot know your pain
or say your sacrifice was worth the cost,
but in the heart of us remains
a goodness that can scarf itself
around you like a warm embrace,
to show that we shall not forget
and you are loved.

St Symphorien Cemetery
i.m. John Parr and George Ellison

Under a gash of green between headstones,
whispers shrive confessions from the soil,

a paired history spliced by coincidence,
the last and the first, the first and last.

Your soldiers' voices ricochet, tongue to tongue,
bullet words of war, a share of confidences

through a century of tortured sleep.
The other's breath has known your cheek,

tasted your mouth, touched your sundered heart,
but the sniper-sharpness in your eyes remains

to ghost away romantic notions
fashioned from an accident of chance.

See instead, between your sleeps,
a truth of corpses stenched in sludge –

the never to return again inheritance of war
and when your almost touching distance is complete,

pray the cost has drenched our consciousness.

FENCED

A fence stretches like a sentence
to the edge of the white page
and your daughter, salient as a hare,
eyes the peopled words until
they fade into their final full stop.

Winter's snow still wraps its cover
around the earth, your child's fingers
ice-burned on the hoarfrost railings
that link from post to post.

She is six years old and not yet
tainted by an anger you have learned to hide,
for she must see beyond the tease of wire
towards those empty pages
she will one day write herself.

Your own unfinished story smoulders
in the greying ash of history now,
its countless epilogues scribed by hands
whose truth is not your own.

Only once you turned to scan
the chapters of the past and know
the future is a fence that you must disassemble
word by word to know its worth
and find a meaning waiting on the other side.

THE REACH

He lays a map upon the table,
fingering their long journey
from the smudge of home
and stabs red-lined borders
that thread like arteries over the creases.
He does not want his children to forget.

His touch finds the place
they should now call home –
this wound on the paper
where their healing can begin
and where every voyage taken
gives promise of a new life.

Yet his head harbours lists
reluctant to recede, grievances
as infinite as time passing in foreign tongues,
remembered losses that may still break him
and an ache for the land left hungry and alone,
withering into a sort of history.

This is their future now, reached
by the single span of a hand across a map.
He will pleat his sorrow into its folds,
pocketing the past in that place
where every road must surely lead
and only the persistent heart can finally know.

CHIMNEY SONG
i.m. Oscar and Valeria Ramirez

From the throat of the chimney, a song,
smoke-trilled in a hearth's open mouth,
a blackbird offering his end of day story
to earth and sky, while here
in my sitting room the world shifts.

On television, a father and child,
his t-shirt backpacking her small frame
suddenly a weight of stones in the current.
Catch of the day.

I muzzle the sound, drown a flow
of blame mouthed from the screen
and in my sitting room catch a blackbird's
song swallowing up the space
between here and the Rio Grande.

FLOATS

I am a photograph in monochrome –
a flipper sucking stubborn
to a naked foot, plastic suicide vest
bottling my chest; death floats, all.
My last swim, my last.

Drag me from the shallows,
discover secrets of my insignificance
bagged around the protest of a drenched throat,
mobile telephone, memory card intact,
leaking the riddle of my shattered history.

For here I am, a thousand fragments
washed in technicolour,
my wanderings weaved frame to frame,
preserved like floaters swimming
in the salty lenses of your eyes.

FOR FRIENDS

Light comes early in the Middle East,
arms stretched out like a hug,
sunbeams swallowing the waned
darkness of the night before.

I am alone here in this beauty,
standing by a window thinking of you,
feeling the distance of your friendship
in the sun's embrace.

But soon this warmth that touches me
will find you too and all will be well,
for the light sustains, knowing
it can always find its way back home.

Tea Boys

The end of a working day
and outside my office
heat can still scorch lungs
as cruelly as an iced intake
of Arctic breath.

Beyond the window,
on a small corner of dust,
I watch your tea boy heads
folded over something
that I cannot see.

Then, like the opening
of a desert flower, you part
to stand in quiet thought,
and at your feet a planting of
three green sprigs.

A plastic water bottle
passes hand to hand,
its trickled contents measured
out as carefully as if it
were a liquid gold.

Here is the simple joy
that ends your day
when all you have is
this one act of love
and know that it's enough.

CALLING

Sound travels stealthily here,
nudged by desert winds
or wing-tucked in flight
over a sapphire sea.

I let it in, breathe the salt taste
through an open doorway
and search for distant minarets
seeking the ears of the faithful.

Strange, too, how a church bell
peals in lingered space,
filling gaps between
the foreignness of each refrain.

Then all at once, in note-merged
harmony, a single song remains,
spilling its oneness to
the journey's end, its call complete.

BACKWARD GLANCING ON A TEHRAN STREET

Turquoise, my colour coat of choice
and yours the emerald green
of half your roots –
the other half a chadored
shadow stretched to fit
a flat screen
back at home.

Here on this Tehran Street,
Khomeini Street,
the black crows
softly trip the light fandango
through a sea of cars
shoaling the three lane surf
forever six lanes deep.

On pavements walk
the kohl-eyed beauty
of the young,
loose slung roosari draped
high on bee hives, nose jobs
sticking – plastered for perfection
(at a western price).

We walk rebellious
in our coloured coats,
the mother-daughter oddity
of us no longer meriting
that whispered backward glance,
for underneath our feet
awakening slowly from its sleep
the Persian tiger stirs.

This Place I Am In

I have come here to where buildings steal the sky,
guzzling clouds by day and stars by night
with unquenchable thirst,
where the throats of cranes
neck together sleek as swans,
long arms finger-touching ribs of steel
a hundred storeys high.

I do not know if this is where I want to be
and think of a place behind me
sucking that same sky into greedy earth,
where ancient quercus leach long in bogs,
guarding their soiled history beneath a century
of stories long forgotten or misunderstood.

I stand upon this bridge between air and earth
and search for answers I can only find myself,
knowing hell cannot be understood
by simply digging down, nor heaven
conquered by a single act of faith.
Yet the present whispers on my skin as soft as prayer
offering up its promises to my reluctant heart,
if only I can let it in.

THE BOILING POINT FOR JAM

She is making jam in the tiny kitchen,
aproned up, thumb-worn spoon in hand,
fingertips browned like nicotine
from plums she'd stoned an hour before.

Through the window she watches him work,
his naked back a tease of muscle-bulk
as axe splits wood, big hands tender on the shaft
with every shlurp of the blade's release.

She adds sugar to the softened fruit,
stirs until its coarseness fuses the pulp.
Then she waits. Outside the sky is bruised with cloud,
the day punished for its obdurate cheerfulness.

He stiffens then, minding something beyond her reach,
and in his stillness she finds the man she knew
who measured time with shrugs and rinsed his days
with promises she could not keep.

Now there is only her raw womb,
the haemorrhage of empty-bellied days
stretching behind her like a vacant sky
and the sweet spit of fruit pricking at her skin.

Yet there is peace in the ordinary:
the boiling point for jam, the quiet release of a latch,
the skirting of his arms about her waist,
the hope that love would always be enough.

FORTY-THREE GRAMS

Too early to name, you were too unfinished
in the womb for anyone to love but me.
At fourteen weeks your stubbed appendages
denied you somehow proper meaning to the world,
yet I imagined then the promise of your touch
and flying fingers someday glancing on piano keys
or toes that curled like leaves in winter after frost.

Behind those swollen sockets
I would never know the colour of your eyes –
if they were brown or blue or hazel like my own.
But somewhere past a sea of years
I watch you dance beneath a saffron sky
on meadows crusted yellow in a summer sun
or hear your footfall whisper soft on winter snow.

Yet now your nearly heartbeat grieves in me,
its pulse the baby miracle I never knew.
Just three and forty grams,
a single letter's weight of life unfinished
in the womb. Too early then to name
so I completed you inside my head
and loved you just the same.

DEATH OF THE SWALLOWS

They dropped where they were
from the garage beams,
wings as slight as any thought
tucked into a fragility of bone and feather.
Three fledglings and their mother,
unnoticed in my haste the day before
when I had closed a door
upon their deaths.

What torpor they retained had been
extinguished in the night,
each unrequited breath a hope
to skim again across an open sky.
So I buried them on feathered backs
their shuttered stares towards the blue
and wings as stiff as bark forever
grounded in terrestrial flight.

BESIDE THE BLACKWATER

Cattle have drunk here,
their pockmarked presence
a suck and pull of plunged hooves
traversing the bank.

Filled tongues mark
a staging post between source and sea
where the river holds her breath
and dark waters hide the treachery
of her under-bellied silt.

Babies perished here,
swallowed by stillness and intent,
fragile bones mere pike-pickings
in the aftermath.

And workhouse mothers
slumped on scoured and bloodied knees
sought penance for a love
surrendered to the river's hold,
wrapped within its embryonic sac.

FULL FRONTAL

I see you across the river,
blinded windows
staring over heron stacks
that shock like bizarre haircuts
in the shallows.

Your mouth bares
its bricked teeth
holed now in decay,
an abscess of innards
spitting rotted detritus
out onto the gravel.

What stories took you here?
Whose eyes observed
from ribboned skylights
in your slated hair?
Or worse, the windows
never seen in their
asylumed anonymity.

I want to comb your hair,
to soap your face
with tenderness,
to smooth the creases
of your desiccating skin,
but I cannot.

For you have seen
in your unblinking stare
across the river's flow
this interloper of the past
and cry again, too late, too late.

DROPPED CALVES, SUCKLERS, WEANLINGS AND STEERS

Their lowing drenches
these redundant pens
and seeps through concrete floors
like blottered ink,
while in a shed
the gavel sleeps,
its gunshot condemnation
silent only after the bidding.

'Dropped calves, sucklers,
weanlings, steers'
the wet-nosed breath of them
hangs still,
its droplets dripping fear
on crusted pats
of meringue-crisp manure.

No sentiment soils
this soulless place,
only the cold stare
of hard men born to it,
their business done
with spit and shake
to seal the deal.

And under a gavel's silence
hums the lament
of those condemned,
carted to slaughter
and a butcher's slab.

PETRICHOR

When the sky cries
open up your face to it
and smell the rain

UNEARTHED

They are skeletoned front to back,
bare of all but what nature rebuffed,
their hands cupped in something
short of prayer.

He nudges her curves,
a puzzle of bones
five thousand years in the making
and imagines her whole again;
heart-keeper, lover, wife,
her ribs singing on his chest,
her breath plumping his cheek.

She knows the bend of his
long legs shadowing,
the lean of his sacrifice on her shoulders,
the graveyard of secrets
stored within their budded palms.
He is the follower,
warder of her solitude.

A coupling of corpses, not yet dust,
years passing across them
like ghosts through open portals,
unearthing more than just a smatter of bone.

Shooting Pigeons

You walked up from the shore
a dog at your heels,
suit pockets spilling nettles
and the sea-spit dully freckled
in your hair. I stood and watched you go,
wanting to pass the time of day
but seeing in your eyes the ghosts of yesteryear
that were no stranger's business,
so I let you be.

The man who shot pigeons
on a Sunday I was told,
in empty warehouse space
where oddities went unremarked
and open rafters' death-bleached
tones of white were spattered scarlet,
while a church bell tolled
and your quiet madness seeped
into those wicker-whitened walls.

They said you'd lost a son
at sea a decade gone and how your sanity
was slowly filched away with every tide
that failed to fetch him home,
but still you walked the shore
in funeral suit of faded blue
picking nettles from the cracks
amongst the sanded rocks,
on every day but one.

I hear that someone found you
stiff and cold, a dead dog at your feet
amongst the feathered sea spray
of a Sunday afternoon,

your pockets finally spilled
with flaccid blooms
of sweet magnolia,
their numbing scent
the ghost you'd finally put to rest.

REAR VIEW MIRROR

At sixty miles an hour you stood no chance –
a thud of skin and fur the ultimate act of being
neither of us could have prophesied.

In the mirror four limbs twitched and jerked
in monochrome and I screamed the whole way home, your
nine lives splayed behind me on the open road.

MISSING

They would find you
three days later,
a smudge on mossy earth,
the mulberry coat
coffin-slouched
to keep you warm,
though an absent heartbeat
was already ceded
in the veins of air and sky
and a residue of smiles
still spittled out along
the pleated seam of your mouth.

A Space of Air and Leaves

I have arrived here from the past,
climbed this tree until its boughs
wishboned their hold upon
my sixty-three years.

I had forgotten the transience of it,
how we are stroked by time and then released,
like leaves lost to an autumn's chill
leaving only a paled cicatrix behind.

The postman comes, spreads letters in the box
and carries on, the open windows of his van
washing out a tune I do not recognise –
it is a small but joyful thing.

I think of television programmes
where falling three feet from a ladder ends in death
or falling thirty from a tree might only bruise your pride,
and know that life is really only random luck.

If we could all just sit in trees, only for a little while,
dangling our legs like children in that space
of air and leaves,
clutching moments as they soak into antiquity.
If only we could all just sit in trees.

CREW CUT

You sit in the seat in front,
as flat headed and neckless
as a nail rammed into
the softness of wood. The scar,
a curved question mark
round your bristled skull
has etched its whiteness into skin
no tattooed ink can imitate.

I long to lay my hand
upon the mystery of it,
feel the crispness of its casing
and let my fingers trace
the secret of your past,
for there are wounds
that need no answer
other than a single touch.

JOHN D.

Man of the hills, still dwelling in a house
that birthed him,
alone among the crags and scraggy fields
that schooled him,
he arrived at my class with the look
of a disapproving uncle.

Man of few words, bubble-wrapped in hat and coat,
a self-imposed quarantine of loneliness
and something else I never fully understood.

Man of seven decades plus, a past indifferent
to the young,
his last remembered writing quilled and inked
when he was just fifteen years old.

Man of beauty, when he smiled that solitary smile
and offered up to me one memory, pencilled shyly
on a crumpled piece of paper.

Man of simple language, where the story of a goat
that followed him to school when he was six,
just broke my heart.

Unmade Bed

Through fraying ends of sleep
I feel your absence
seeping through the coldness
of the sheets.
The smell of you
still shelters in their folds,
while dented on the pillow
your presence lingers like a bruise
that aches of memory,
surrendering itself to time.

THE COLOUR OF AN ORANGE

I tried to show you once, in words,
the colour of an orange –

a Tunisian sun drying on the horizon of the earth's curve,
a hunched back in a Guantanamo cell,
the underbelly of a low-cost aircraft flying out of Belfast.

Yes, you said,
but what colour is an orange?

The sadness of losing the sun's warmth, I said,
the hopelessness of unrequited prayer,
the expectation of exploring the unknown.

Very good, you said,
but what colour is an orange?

So I tried,
the heat that follows shadow,
a smile for nothing,
a reach from your blind eyes to the sun,

and then you knew.

Lay of the Land

This is where the land lies –

in a school assembly hall,
the words of children chattering
from wall displays,
a wish of rainbows smiling
optimism on A4 sheets.

But in a booth of anti-time
voters pencil numbers
on a page, delivering us back
to the land of our forefathers
and where the land lay then.

THIS TRUE AND LOVELY THING

Day enters with a shrug,
effortless under bedroom window blinds,
its residue of darkness scraped bare
from the night that has gone before.

A child slumbers, her prayers
soused within the walls of sleep –
words learned by rote to dissipate the harmings
of a world no longer certain of itself.

Yet the day still comes
and prayers of children continue their calling
in a new dawn, swelling like a full heart
with the promise of some true and lovely thing

only now a sigh away.

TAKEN

For months, a mile or more his legs took him,
walking the hedgerows to seek her memory
amongst the blackthorn and the meadowsweet.
It was the kind of madness grief makes of a man,
scorching his eyes, invading the wounds of his heart.

They had come in stealth, filching his dead wife
from where she lingered in dressing table drawers
and trinket boxes long ago lost of polish and key.
A handkerchief that owned her smell, the string of pearls
she wore on holidays or with her Sunday best.

He found her bible snagged in the blackthorn,
a discarded spoil of her stolen life, the list of family
deaths and births on a back page discernible
in copperplate and pallid ink,
singing her long history
in the hidden value of the words.

Now he weeps his loneliness into their cold sheets,
the lost smell of her too high a cost for none
but himself to know, as he wonders at the value
of her wedding ring on a stranger's finger,
or the price of her worthless pearls languishing
in another's dressing table drawer.

WAITING

Swallows spark kisses on power lines,
eyes keenly south, the dregs of summer
on their feathered backs

and in the garden beech trees
robe in auburn, green and gold,
fragile leaf buds coveted until the spring.

Earth's lungs breathe their
circadian rhythm underfoot,
yesterday consigned to memory while

tomorrow hangs unscripted in the wings.
For there is only this, the pulse of the present
swiftly swallowed up within a single breath.

FLAT

Something important inside of me has expired,
my gunged parts choked of the life they owned
when once I owned the life I thought I had.

Something terrible has filched away my kindness
without the courtesy of asking and laid it
on display in a place unfilled and unfathomable.

On nights before mornings I think of this
as sleep takes refuge in walls that creak and sway
with indifference and will not let me through.

I am here scavenging for my life like a hunted child,
heart full of innocent hope, the rest of me silently
just getting on and getting on and getting on.

BACK TO THE ISLAND

Here you are,
returned across the wild Atlantic,
sixty years a ghost from laws
that finally bullied you away.
Laws marked only by
a hunching skulk of hedge,
hog-maned on wasted hillsides
and an ocean's shrugged indifference
to the coiling loneliness
that purged this island of its lifeblood.

Here you are,
bulge-backed in old man clothes,
squelching the sponged earth again like a child,
as history scours your bones
to seek revenge for the unrepentant
sin of your abandonment.
Sixty years of stubborn ocean
scorching its guilt upon your soul
has claimed its recompense
and finally trawled you home.

A QUIET SUSURRATION OF THE HEART
for Emma Gonzalez

A girl scatters names
into the silence,
spattering them like buckshot –
remembering.

Her stare is hollowed grief,
her mouth the shrapnel
of unalterable witness,
but her breath, her breath
is a quiet susurration
of the heart.

Stoneman Douglas
Six minutes and twenty seconds –
Remembering.

Remembering them all.

BULLY'S ACRE
burial place of the poor of Clougher 1852–1949

The dead still live here in stifled ghosts
shifting beneath a weight of sorrows,

while under these unhallowed yews
the paupers sigh a song of anonymity,

each stolen breath gathered in the
fist of the wind and crushed to dust.

WATERMARK
i.m. Seamus Heaney

So the sleán has ceased its cut
and the soft bogs of Ireland
soak in tears from some impenetrable loss.

Out of the land they seep
their salted wetness surfacing
like moisture pearls

to merge and hold, and merge again;
a river coursing free
from source to open sea

and on its tide
a legacy of words
diminishing the keening in their wake

as the imprint of your watermark endures –
remembered, loved and missed,
for us; the lover's stamp,

your final kiss.

GARDEN

Edward, you are the holly,
pulled by the roots from a memory hedge
to grow again in different soil.
Away from the tree that claimed you,
away, away from that garden of reminders
where your mother's pain
looked out upon the thief
that had stolen you. But I want to show her
the roots of you now. Here,
where underneath the ground
they are strong and reaching
and your leaves never shrivel
in the blind winds of winter
after all this time.

Father, you are the bendy beech,
drawn from a Fermanagh bog, a sapling
twisting your resistance into a foreign home
where I transported you, just
to have your presence close.
At your feet a boot of snowdrops
kicks the winter into spring, and
from your branches, fingertips of bud await
a summer's touch before they flare.
And when I listen, cheek pressed close
against the roughness of your bark,
I hear the rising sap of who you are
speaking to me through
the quiet earth.

Mother, the rose. How could you not be?
Grown from a slip you'd slipped
from somewhere else,
your blossoms bleeding pink,

and red and white
with edges crinkled like
the smile that rested
easily upon your mouth.
Rosa Mundi, there against the garden seat
where stroppy summer sunshine
warms your climb in fits and starts
and where a thrush's egg
nests unobserved, a soporific embryo
of mother scent.

Friends – you know who you are;
sessile oak and silver birch,
willows, weeping their remembrance
in an autumn helicopter flight
of seeds across a lawn.
I planted you with care,
dug the beds you lie in deep
and named you for
the losses in my heart;
Kindness, Beauty, Loyalty and Love,
friendships living on with
every rising of a morning sun,
and all of you the light that greets
the coming day.

Garden, necropolis of planted souls,
shaped only from the clay
of a forgotten field, I have
seen you in your nudity and
best attire. For nature's fickleness
will dress you how she will,
decay of leaf and blossom mulched
to clothe her growing needs, and

every lovely thing that has
endured must someday die.
But in between the then and now
remains those second chances
offering up their promises
towards the light.

YOU'RE BEAUTIFUL

say it to the person who saved you
by saying it
and didn't even know

say it at the moon to borrow its beauty
for yourself
just by noticing

say it because that's what the world
might become if
we said it more often

say it to yourself
when it's not
who you are facing in the mirror

say it even if the one
you say it to
wounds with their indifference

say it out loud
like a poem learned at school –
it will live in you afterwards

say it in a lonely room
for walls have ears
and sound travels fastest through solids

say it for nothing
because something offered freely
is blessed with more than what we cannot see

say it so that nobody
can hear – then let it go
and see how far a fragile thought can fly

say it to the one who saved you
by saying it
and didn't even know

you're beautiful.

ACKNOWLEDGEMENTS

I would like to thank publisher Alan Hayes for his belief in my poetry throughout these strangest of times.

I wish to thank the Arts Council of Northern Ireland for their support, and also fellow poet Damian Smyth for his encouragement and guidance.

I am grateful to my family and friends for their unfailing support over the many years it has taken to gather this collection together. My sister, Jean, has been the mainstay of my writing.

Gratitude to Eileen Casey, Ger Reidy and Geraldine Mitchell for their generous words and faith in my poetry.

Thank you to artist Emma Barone for the use of her artwork on the cover of this collection.

Thanks to the editors of the anthologies and journals where some of these poems, or versions of, first appeared: *Skylight 47*/*North West Words*/*Poethead*/*Live Encounters*/*Skein* (Templar Poetry)/*Abridged*/*Hennessy New Irish Writing, The Irish Times*/ *A New Ulster*/*Waterford Teachers' Centre Anthology*/*Persian Sugar in English Tea*/*CAP Seamus Heaney Anthology*/Poetry Day Ireland audio poems/*Where are you from?*/*4X4*/*Willawaw Journal* (USA)/*Bangor Literary Journal*/Lagan Online audio poems/*The Lea-Green Down*/*Dodging the Rain*/*Fresh Air Poetry*/ *Blackbough Poetry Anthology*/*Pendemic*.

'The Big Freeze', winner of the Westival International Poetry Competition 2018; 'Words', runner up, the Blackwater International Poetry Competition 2019; 'Murder in the First', runner up, Roscommon Poetry Competition 2018; 'Kitchen Comforts'/'Is This What I Do?' Hennessy New Irish Writing, *The Irish Times*, October 2015; 'Death of the Swallows', highly commended/shortlisted for the Wells Poetry Competition 2019, Westival International Poetry Competition; 'The Boiling Point for Jam', highly commended, Welsh Poetry Competition 2018; 'The Colour of an Orange', commended, Roscommon Poetry Competition 2018; 'The Big Tree', shortlisted for The Bangor Poetry Competition 2019; 'Forty-three Grams', Winner of Listowel 'Originals' Competition.

About the Author

Lynda Tavakoli, a retired special needs teacher, lives in Baillies Mills, County Down where she facilitates an adult creative writing class and is a tutor for the Community Arts Partnership, Seamus Heaney Awards for schools. She presently divides her time between Northern Ireland and Oman, where her Persian husband works. A poet, fiction writer and freelance journalist, Lynda's writing has been widely published in the UK, Ireland, the US and the Middle East.

Lynda has written two novels, *Attachment* and *Of Broken Things,* and a short story anthology, *Under a Cold White Moon* (David James Publishing). She is a contributing writer for *The Belfast Telegraph* and *Slugger O'Toole* and had her work broadcast on BBC Radio Ulster, RTÉ Sunday Miscellany and NVTV. Other successes include the *Mail on Sunday* Novel Award and the Mencap Short Story Competition.

She has been winner of both poetry and short story prizes in Listowel and the Westival International Poetry Prize. In 2019 she was runner-up in The Blackwater International Poetry Competition and Roscommon Poetry Competition. Her poems have been published in *The Irish Times* (New Irish Writing) and been translated into Farsi for the anthologies *Where are you from?* and *Persian Sugar in English Tea.*

This is her debut poetry collection.